— BOOK ONE —

VEDANTA IN PLAIN ENGLISH

WHO AM I, REALLY?

An Ancient Guide to Self-knowledge

DANIEL MCKENZIE

Broken Tusk Press

Copyright © 2025 Daniel McKenzie

ISBN: 979-8-9897339-4-1

www.thebrokentusk.com

CONTENTS

PART 4: LIVING THE KNOWLEDGE

APPENDIX

Series Preface

Vedanta in Plain English was created to make the ancient insights of Vedanta accessible in clear, everyday language. Vedanta, the non-dual wisdom tradition, asks the oldest question a mind can ask — *Who am I?* — and answers it not with belief but with reason. It examines experience the way a scientist examines nature: by testing what is constant amid change.

These books are written for readers who are curious about consciousness but prefer clarity to mysticism. Each volume explores one facet of the inquiry, using observation, psychology, and logic to uncover insights that the ancient texts reached by other means. No Sanskrit is required. No devotion, rituals, or systems of belief.

What you'll find here are explanations meant to be verified in your own experience. The point is not to persuade but to illuminate what has always been true.

PART 1

THE PROBLEM OF IDENTITY

We live on autopilot, mistaking reaction for life.

CHAPTER 1

WHY WE'RE CONFUSED

It's not your fault. It's been hidden from you this whole time.

You wake up and reach for the phone before your eyes have fully opened. The day begins in other people's lives — messages, headlines, photos, alerts. By the time you've finished scrolling, your own life feels like something happening off-screen. You call it staying informed, but really you're being programmed. It's not malicious, it's mechanical.

And the strangest part is, you don't even know what's missing, or why. You move from day to day chasing what you like and dodging what you don't, never stopping to ask what the entire system is running on top of. The job, the relationships, the screen time, the ambitions. Everything hums along on invisible software you've never examined.

You assume you're the one in control, steering through life, but really you're being run by an algorithm you didn't write. And that algorithm has one simple line of code: Seek pleasure, avoid pain.

The program shows up everywhere: in the urge to check notifications, in the quiet panic of being left out, in the endless pursuit of "better."

We chase success because failure hurts.
We chase love because loneliness burns.
We chase peace because our own minds are noisy.

The Auto-Pilot Life

The code works well enough to keep the species alive, but not to keep you sane.

It drives the whole machine: scrolling for dopamine, working for recognition, buying for comfort, arguing for validation — refresh, repeat, sleep, and start again. We call it living. It's really reacting.

Most people never notice, because the system rewards busyness and punishes silence. The moment you stop running, you feel the weight of everything you've been outrunning. So you start running again.

Eventually, the body tires and the mind grows suspicious. You begin to notice that every high collapses into a low, every victory breeds the next pursuit. The chase keeps you busy, but not fulfilled. It's at that moment — when effort itself feels empty — that the real search begins.

No one told you there's an alternative. That's the
secret Vedanta begins with — not a promise of
heaven, but the revelation that you've confused the
mechanism for yourself.

The Hidden Mechanism

If you watch closely, you'll see how predictable it all
is.

A compliment appears > you brighten.
A criticism lands > you contract.
A desire whispers > you obey.
A fear flares > you flee.

It's like a marionette show where every string is
pulled by pleasure or pain, and the puppet insists, "I'm
free." The puppet isn't bad; it just thinks every twitch
is a choice. It doesn't know what's holding it up.

The Cost of Unawareness

The price of running the program is exhaustion.

You can keep it going for years — decades even — but there's always that background hum of dissatisfaction. You try to drown it out with music, work, spirituality, wine, or self-help, but it keeps coming back. Because the problem isn't in the content of life; it's in the context.

You've never been shown how to look behind the screen, to see the awareness in which the entire drama is playing. Vedanta doesn't say the world is wrong. It says you've been looking from the wrong side of the lens.

The First Crack

Once in a while, the loop falters. You catch yourself mid-scroll and wonder, What am I even looking for?

You get what you wanted and feel the high dissolve faster than expected. You see someone else suffering and, for a second, the walls between you vanish.

Those moments are cracks in the shell. They hint that something vast and steady lies underneath the noise — a field of awareness that doesn't come and go with circumstance.

That's the first real clue. Not philosophy, not belief.

Just a glimpse of something that doesn't move while everything else does.

The Invitation

You can ignore the cracks and keep running. Most people do. Or you can pause and ask the one question that ends every loop: *Who's the one being pushed and pulled by all this?*

That's where Vedanta starts. Not in belief, but in genuine curiosity. Not in worship, but in looking.

Because the real problem was never the chase. It was never knowing who was doing the chasing.

We mistake the costume for the actor, the story for the self.

CHAPTER 2

WHO WE THINK WE ARE

Who's running all this?

It sounds simple — just a single question — but it's the one most people spend their entire lives avoiding. Instead, we build elaborate identities to protect the assumption that we already know who we are. "I'm a parent, a professional, a friend, a citizen, a spiritual person." The words change, but the hidden message stays the same: This is me. Don't mess with it.

From Vedanta's point of view, this identity — the one you defend, improve, promote, and worry about — isn't the real you. It's a construct, a useful costume for moving through the world, but not the actor wearing it. It's the surface "I," not the witnessing one.

The Layered Self

When you say "I," what exactly are you referring to?

If someone criticizes your work, you feel attacked. If someone praises your taste, you feel pleased. But the

"I" that responds to these things isn't stable. It shifts with circumstance. At work, "I" is the competent professional. At home, "I" is the partner or parent. Online, "I" is the curated avatar with better lighting.

We swap these masks constantly, and each insists it's the real one. That's why life feels so fragile. The moment a mask cracks — when we lose status, health, youth, or love — we feel personally diminished, as though something essential has been taken from us.

But notice: the awareness watching those changes never diminishes. The same awareness that knew your five-year-old body, your teenage body, and your adult body is still here, unchanged. The forms altered; the knower didn't.

The Borrowed "I"

In early childhood, the sense of "I" forms through reflection — literally. You learn who you are through other people's reactions. Parents, teachers, peers, culture all hold up mirrors that say, You're good, you're bad, you're pretty, you're lazy, you're special, you're ordinary. Over time, you internalize those mirrors and call the result "me."

The trouble is that every mirror shows a slightly

different image. When you live by reflection alone, you're always dependent on the next reaction to feel real. Praise inflates you; criticism punctures you. Vedanta calls this dependence the "borrowed self," a personality built from other people's perceptions.

It's not evil; it's just incomplete. The borrowed self can navigate the world, but it can never find peace, because it's always negotiating its worth.

The Problem of Ownership

We tend to identify with whatever feels close. When you say "my hand," it's clear you're not the hand — you have it. But when you say "my mind" or "my feelings," the ownership line blurs. It's as if the mind and body move into the house and start getting mail addressed to "Self."

We talk as if the thoughts belong to us: I'm anxious, I'm angry, I'm enlightened. But thoughts simply appear, stay a while, and pass. If they were truly yours, you'd be able to control them — choose only the pleasant ones, discard the rest. The fact that you can't shows you're not the thinker; you're the observer of thought.

The same goes for the body. You can influence it, but

not command it. It grows, ages, and eventually stops
— all without consulting you. Yet something constant
remains through every stage, something aware of
every change. That unchanging witness is closer to the
truth of "I."

The Witness Behind the Masks

Every night, in deep sleep, all your roles vanish. The
mind quiets, the body rests, the world disappears.
And yet you wake up and say, "I slept well." How
could you know that if "you" were absent?

Because even in the absence of personality, awareness
remains. That's the witness — pure consciousness
— not doing anything, not owning anything, simply
being. It was there before you opened your eyes this
morning, and it will be there after your final breath.

This awareness isn't something you achieve; it's what
you've always been. The masks, roles, and labels are
temporary overlays, useful for playing the human
game. But the player isn't the costume.

A Subtle Shift

When this understanding deepens, nothing dramatic

happens. You still play your roles — parent, profes-sional, friend — but you no longer mistake them for your essence. The world keeps spinning; you stop clinging.

Ironically, life becomes lighter, not heavier. You can laugh at yourself more easily because you know the self you're laughing at isn't ultimately you. You stop needing everyone to agree with your story. You still act, still care, but from freedom, not compulsion.

This is the first fruit of Vedantic knowledge: not a cosmic vision, but a quiet shift in identification. From the borrowed "I" to the witnessing Self. It's simple, but it changes everything.

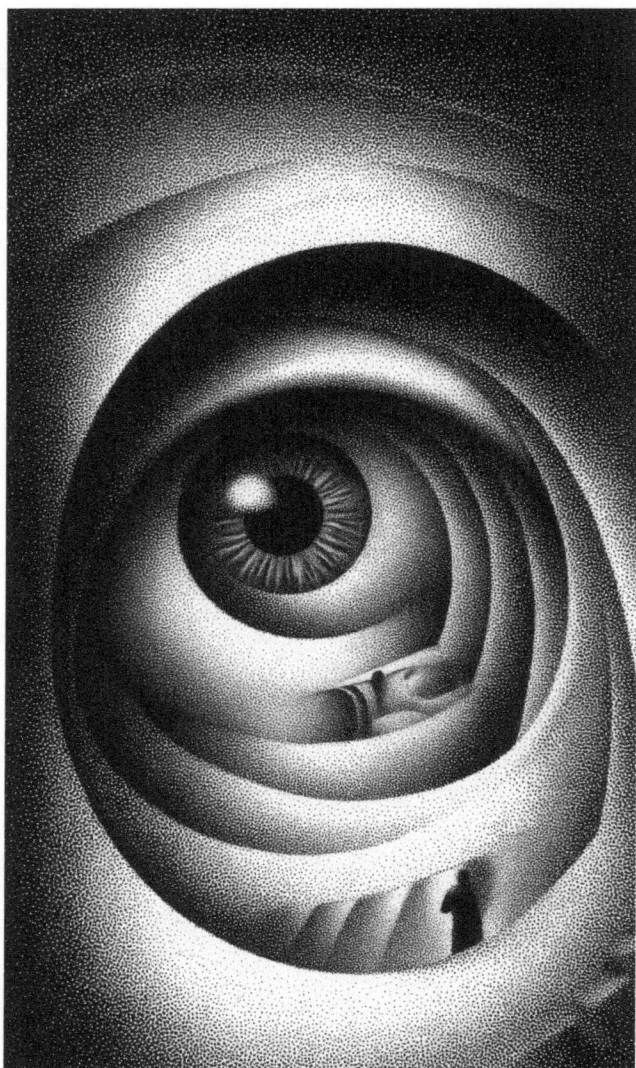

The oldest question still waits for
an answer that doesn't move.

CHAPTER 3

THE ANCIENT QUESTION

Every culture has asked it. Every seeker, skeptic, and wanderer eventually stumbles upon it: *Who am I?*

Three small words that sound almost childish, yet hide the oldest riddle in human history. The moment you stop taking your identity for granted, this question appears like a quiet echo beneath every thought and feeling. It's the pulse of philosophy, the seed of religion, and the one inquiry that no technology, no therapy, and no ideology has ever managed to answer for you.

The Oldest Question in the World

Long before psychology or neuroscience, the sages of the Upanishads turned this question inward. Sitting in stillness, they asked not about the gods above but about the awareness within. What is the knower of experience? What remains when the roles, the body, and the mind fall silent?

Their conclusion was radical: the answer to *Who am*

I? is not something to be discovered in the world, but something to be recognized in oneself.

In the *Brihadaranyaka Upanishad,* Yajnavalkya tells his student, "You cannot see the seer of seeing." The *Chandogya Upanishad* calls it *That thou art.* Each text points in the same direction: the one who asks the question is the very truth being sought.

The Modern Search

Our era hasn't stopped asking; it's just changed vocabulary. We frame the question in psychological or scientific terms: *What defines consciousness? What makes me unique?*

We analyze brain scans, build personality tests, and debate nature versus nurture. We compare childhood traumas, take mindfulness courses, and chase "authentic living." All of it is sincere, yet most of it keeps the focus outward. We try to map the territory instead of realizing we're the field itself.

Self-help, in particular, has made a business out of keeping the question open. "Who am I?" becomes a lifelong brand, complete with workshops and hashtags. But Vedanta suggests something more daring: the question can be answered — not by finding a better self, but by understanding the self that's never changed.

Turning the Question Inward

When Vedanta says, "Turn within," it doesn't mean stare at your navel or retreat from the world. It means reverse the direction of inquiry.

Normally, attention flows outward toward objects, thoughts, sensations. The mind says, I see, I think, I feel, and assumes the "I" is the doer behind them. Vedanta asks: what if "I" is not the doer but the witness of doing?

Just as the eyes can't see themselves, the self can't be objectified. You can't point to it, describe it, or conceptualize it, you can only be it. The practice of Vedanta isn't about building a stronger identity; it's about discovering the awareness that allows every identity to appear and disappear without loss.

Belief vs Knowledge

Many seekers stop at belief. They collect ideas about enlightenment, read sacred texts, attend retreats, and decide, *I believe this is true*. But belief still lives in the mind; it can strengthen or fade.

Knowledge is different. Knowledge ends the search. When you know fire burns, you don't need faith to avoid the flame. When you know who you are — not intellectually but through direct recognition — the compulsion to seek dissolves.

Vedanta calls this *Self-knowledge*. It's not mystical. It's the clear understanding that awareness itself is your nature, that you were never the limited person you took yourself to be.

The Upanishads never say, "You will become the Self." They say, *You are That*. The teaching simply removes the ignorance that made you believe otherwise.

The Threshold of Inquiry

When the question "Who am I?" is asked with sincerity, something subtle shifts. It's no longer an intellectual puzzle but an invitation. The mind quiets, the old assumptions lose authority, and awareness begins to notice itself.

This is where Vedanta truly begins — not with dogma or ritual, but with curiosity purified of every agenda. The next chapters will show how the tradition

uses scripture, logic, and guidance to unfold this recognition step by step.

For now, it's enough to feel the question itself working on you — simple, ancient, and indestructible.

Who am I?

The first and final question.

PART 2

THE METHOD OF INQUIRY

Vedanta doesn't give you beliefs.
It removes what hides the truth.

CHAPTER 4

WHAT VEDANTA IS (AND ISN'T)

The word *Vedanta* can sound intimidating. It carries the weight of an ancient language, wrapped in mystery and sandalwood smoke. To the casual ear, it might sound like a religion, a philosophy, or another exotic path among thousands. It's none of those things. And a little of each.

Not a Belief System

Let's start with what it's not. Vedanta is not something to believe in. Belief asks you to accept something you don't yet know. Vedanta asks you to look directly at what you already know, but have never examined.

It doesn't tell you what to think; it teaches you how to see. Its job is not to give you new experiences, but to reinterpret the ones you already have.

When people first encounter Vedanta, they sometimes assume it's another flavor of Eastern mysticism or a cousin of yoga philosophy. In truth, it's a means of knowledge — a structured method for removing ignorance about who you are. The Sanskrit word *anta* means "end," and *veda* means "knowledge." So, *Vedanta* literally means "the end of knowledge," or more precisely, the culmination of the search for truth.

A Mirror, Not a Microscope

Vedanta doesn't work like science or psychology. Science studies what you can observe. Psychology studies the mind that does the observing. Vedanta studies the knower — that which is aware of both.

That's why it's called a mirror teaching. A microscope shows you something you couldn't see before; a mirror shows you what was always there. When you look into a clean mirror, nothing new appears. Only the ignorance that hid your reflection is removed.

Vedanta doesn't create realization. It reveals what is already the case.

The Threefold Method

Like any precise method, Vedanta relies on certain

tools. Traditionally, there are three:

Scripture (Shruti) — the words of those who have already seen. The Upanishads, the *Bhagavad Gita*, and other texts act as the blueprint. They are not sacred because they ask for worship, but because they point reliably toward truth.

Reason (Yukti) — logic and inquiry. Vedanta never asks you to suspend intellect; it uses reasoning to confirm what the scripture reveals. If something cannot hold up to logic, it's not Vedanta.

Teacher (Acharya) — not a guru in the pop-spiritual sense, but someone who knows the methodology and can guide the student step by step. A qualified teacher keeps you from getting lost in abstraction or ego.

These three together — scripture, reason, and teacher — form a triangle of clarity. Remove one, and the structure collapses into belief or confusion.

Qualifications of the Seeker

The teaching is open to everyone, but the student must be ready. The texts describe this readiness through four qualifications, though they're less mystical than they sound:

Discrimination (viveka) — the ability to tell what's real and lasting from what's temporary and changing.

Dispassion (vairagya) — freedom from blind attachment to pleasure or fear of pain.

Discipline (shatsampatti) — a collection of inner strengths like calmness, focus, endurance, and trust.

Desire for freedom (mumukshutva) — the sincere longing to be free from limitation.

You don't need these perfected to begin; you cultivate them as you go. The important thing is sincerity — the sense that you've tried everything else, and now you're ready to look directly.

Not a Religion

Religion begins with devotion; Vedanta begins with inquiry. Religion asks you to believe in God; Vedanta asks, *Who is the believer?* Religion often divides the sacred from the profane; Vedanta says nothing is outside the whole.

That doesn't make religion wrong, it simply has a different function. Religion prepares the heart. Vedanta liberates the mind. Many great teachers say religion is the kindergarten, and Vedanta is the graduate school of spiritual understanding.

Why It Still Matters

You might wonder how something born thousands of years ago could possibly speak to our modern confusion. But human nature hasn't changed. The same mind that once sat under a banyan tree is now sitting under fluorescent light, scrolling on a phone. The desires are newer; the restlessness is the same.

Vedanta endures because it's not about culture or belief. It's about the structure of experience itself. It asks the same question now as it did then: *If you are aware of your thoughts, can you really be your thoughts?*

That's not an ancient riddle. That's the starting point of freedom.

The Beginning of the End

Vedanta doesn't end the world. It ends confusion about it. It's the rare teaching that doesn't promise transformation, it promises clarity.

You don't become divine; you realize you were never

anything less. That's the quiet revolution Vedanta brings. Not fireworks. Not ecstasy. Just a deep, steady knowing that leaves nothing to fix.

You are not what appears in the mirror.
You are the light that reveals it.

CHAPTER 5

THE MIRROR OF CONSCIOUSNESS

If you close your eyes for a moment, the world disappears. Open them, and it rushes back in — a flood of color, shape, motion, sound. Everything you experience seems to come to you. But what is the "you" it comes to?

The Seer and the Seen

Vedanta begins its inquiry with a simple observation: whatever you can observe, you are not.

You can observe the body, so you are not the body. You can observe thoughts, so you are not your thoughts. You can observe feelings, so you are not your feelings.

The one who observes — the seer — is distinct from the seen. The seen is changing, temporary, dependent. The seer is constant, silent, and aware.

This distinction sounds obvious, yet we rarely live

from it. We say my body, my mind, my emotions, but somehow forget the "my" that owns them. We live as if the passing cloud were the sky itself.

Awareness in Disguise

Right now, as you read these words, awareness is present. It's not the words, not the meanings, not the thoughts they trigger. It's the field in which all of that appears. Awareness doesn't need to announce itself. It doesn't say, I am aware. It simply is.

When you notice a sound, awareness is there. When you fail to notice, awareness is still there. The content changes; the presence never does.

The mind borrows light from this awareness the way the moon borrows light from the sun. Without that borrowed light, there would be no thought, no perception, no experience at all.

The Clean Mirror

Vedanta calls this awareness *the witness* — not a person watching from somewhere, but the pure capacity to know.

When the mind is calm, it functions like a clean mirror: it reflects the world accurately and lets the light of awareness shine through. When it's disturbed by emotion or desire, the reflection warps.

But notice — no matter how distorted the image becomes, the mirror itself is never stained. Anger, joy, sorrow, fear: they pass across its surface and vanish. Awareness remains untouched.

You don't have to purify awareness; you only need to stop confusing the dirt on the mirror for the mirror itself.

You Are the Light, Not the Lamp

Think of awareness as light and the mind as the lamp. The lamp can flicker, dim, or even break, but the light itself is independent.

When you say, *I'm tired, I'm anxious, I'm happy,* what you really mean is: the lamp is flickering this way right now. The light hasn't changed.

This realization doesn't dismiss emotion or dull experience, it frees them. Joy can be full, grief can be real, and yet something in you remains steady, untouched.

The mistake isn't in feeling; it's in believing the feeling defines you.

Knowing the Knower

At first glance, it seems impossible to "know" awareness. How can the eye see itself?

Vedanta answers: awareness doesn't need another instrument to know, it is self-revealing.

You never have to look for consciousness because it's what's looking. You never have to make awareness happen because nothing happens without it.

The mind can report awareness, but it can't produce it. It's the witness that enables every report.

A Quiet Experiment

Try this: Sit quietly for ten seconds and notice everything that changes — sounds, sensations, thoughts.

Now, notice what doesn't change.

That still presence, that background clarity — that's the real "I." You can't describe it because description itself arises within it. But you can recognize it instantly once pointed out. And once recognized, it's impossible to unsee.

The Shift of Identity

When this insight matures, something profound yet ordinary occurs: the center of gravity moves.

Life continues — emails, errands, traffic — but the sense of "me" starts to loosen. You stop being the actor lost in the play and realize you're the screen on which the play appears.

That's not detachment; it's intimacy without entanglement. You can love fully, act clearly, and rest deeply because you're no longer confusing the passing with the permanent.

The Mirror Reveals Itself

Vedanta's purpose isn't to give you new experiences of light. It's to show you that you are the light.

The world, the mind, and the senses are reflections — beautiful, intricate, sometimes chaotic — but reflections all the same.

Once you recognize yourself as the mirror, life stops being a chase for clearer images. You can finally rest, not in ignorance, but in knowledge.

The waves depend on the ocean,
but the ocean depends on nothing.

CHAPTER 6

DISCRIMINATING THE REAL FROM THE UNREAL

Everything you know appears and disappears.

Thoughts, sensations, memories, even the body — each arises, lingers for a while, then fades. And yet, something never comes or goes. That "something" is not a mystery; it's the one thing you never lose sight of: awareness itself.

The Practice of Discrimination

In Vedanta, this ability to tell what is constant from what is changing is called discrimination (viveka).

It's not moral judgment. It's clarity.

Look at any object around you: a cup, a cloud, your own reflection. Every one of them depends on something else for existence. The cup depends on clay, the cloud on water vapor, the reflection on a mirror. But the clay doesn't depend on the cup; the mirror doesn't depend on the image.

When you trace anything back far enough, you find a substratum that doesn't depend on anything else. Vedanta calls that substratum Reality — that which always is.

What Is Real?

The tradition defines the real as that which is always present and never changes.

If something comes and goes, it's not fully real. It's *apparently real.*

You can dream of flying, and in the dream the sky feels solid. But when you wake up, the entire experience vanishes. From the waking standpoint, the dream was only apparent — it appeared but had no independent existence.

From the standpoint of awareness, the waking world is the same. It appears vividly, but only within consciousness. It depends on consciousness, while consciousness depends on nothing.

The Two Orders of Reality

To make this practical, Vedanta distinguishes between

two levels:

The Absolute (satya): what never changes
— awareness.

The Apparent (mithya): what seems to change —
body, mind, world.

Both exist, but in different ways. Just as the wave
cannot exist apart from water, the world cannot exist
apart from awareness.

This doesn't mean the world is an illusion like a hal-
lucination; it means it's dependent. The error lies in
taking the dependent as the independent — mistaking the shadow for the substance.

Dependence and Independence

Every experience depends on awareness to be known.

Awareness depends on nothing to be itself.

If you say, "I'm aware of my thoughts," awareness is present. If you say, "I'm not aware of anything," awareness is still present — it's aware of the
blankness.

That's the test of reality: what remains when everything else changes.

When this discrimination becomes steady, the world doesn't vanish; its grip does. You can love, work, and play without confusion because you know what's real and what's just passing scenery.

Seeing Through the Movie

Imagine watching a film. The images move, the story unfolds, emotions rise and fall, but the screen never flinches. The screen isn't inside the story; the story is inside the screen.

You don't need to destroy the movie to recognize the screen. You just need to know what you're looking at.

Vedanta trains this shift in vision. It's not about withdrawing from the world, but about seeing the order of reality clearly: dependent appearance resting on independent awareness.

Freedom Through Clarity

The mind's suffering comes from reversal. We treat the temporary as permanent, the dependent as independent, the apparent as absolute.

When we reverse that error through discrimination, something remarkable happens. Freedom doesn't need to be achieved; it's recognized as already here.

The body can age, the mind can change, relationships can begin and end, but the reality that illumines them remains untouched.

That's why Vedanta says liberation isn't about gaining anything new. It's about seeing clearly what was true all along.

PART 3

THE DISCOVERY

You have a body and a mind,
but you are the awareness that own neither.

CHAPTER 7

THE SELF IS NOT THE BODY OR MIND

You've said "my body" your whole life. "My hand hurts." "My stomach's upset." "My face looks tired."

Even language admits that the body belongs to you.

So who is the "you" the body belongs to?

The Body is Known

Close your eyes. Feel the body sitting, breathing, pulsing. You know its sensations — the warmth in your palms, the heartbeat in your chest. But anything you can know is an object of awareness, not awareness itself.

The body is known. Therefore, the body cannot be the knower. When you were a child, the body looked different. When you sleep, it disappears from view. You say, "I was a baby," "I grew up," "I got older." That means you — the witness — were present through all those changes.

The body has never once said, I am. It's awareness
that says that, through it.

The Senses Are Known

The same logic applies to the senses. You know sight,
sound, taste, touch, and smell. You know when they're
functioning and when they're not.

Sometimes you see clearly, sometimes you don't
Sometimes you hear music, sometimes silence. You're
aware of both — the sound and the absence of sound.

So you can't be the hearing or the seeing, because
both come and go within your presence.

The senses belong to you, but you don't belong to
them.

The Mind Is Known

Thoughts rise like bubbles and vanish just as quickly.

"I'm hungry." "I'm anxious." "I'm planning tomorrow."

They seem personal, but watch closely — they arrive
uninvited and leave without warning.

If you were the mind, you'd have perfect control over it.

You'd choose only uplifting thoughts, never the painful ones.

But the mind behaves more like weather than a servant. It moves by its own conditioning, its own momentum.

You are aware of the thoughts, which means you are not the thoughts.

The same goes for emotion. Anger flares and fades. Joy comes and passes. Each one is witnessed by the same still presence that never changes.

The Five Layers

Vedanta describes the person as wrapped in five layers or "sheaths":

The physical sheath — the body of food (*annamaya kosha*).

The energy sheath — breath and life force (*pranamaya kosha*).

The mental sheath — thoughts and emotions (*mano-maya kosha*).

The intellect sheath — reason and understanding (*vijnanamaya kosha*).

The bliss sheath — deep sleep and subtle joy (*anandamaya kosha*).

Each sheath can be known, which means each is an object. The Self is not any of them.

You can't be the clothing you wear, no matter how tightly it fits.

The Witness Beyond the Layers

The one constant through all these layers is awareness.

It doesn't need a body to exist; it simply uses the body as an instrument of experience. It doesn't need the mind to think; it illumines thought when thought appears.

When you understand this directly — not just intellectually — the sense of "I" begins to shift.

You no longer feel trapped inside the body; the

body happens in you. You no longer feel defined by
thought; thought happens in you.

Not a Denial, but a Discovery

Vedanta doesn't ask you to reject the body or the
mind. They're necessary, functional, and beautiful
parts of the total. It simply asks you not to confuse
the instruments with the player.

You are the awareness in which body, senses, and
mind appear and disappear. You were here before the
first thought this morning, and you'll be here after the
last one tonight.

Even in deep sleep, when the mind is absent,
you remain. The witness was never absent, only
unrecognized.

The Beginning of True Seeing

When you see this clearly, fear begins to fall away.

What can death take from you if you were never the
body? What can failure take from you if you were
never the mind?

Freedom begins not by escaping the world, but by understanding what was never bound.

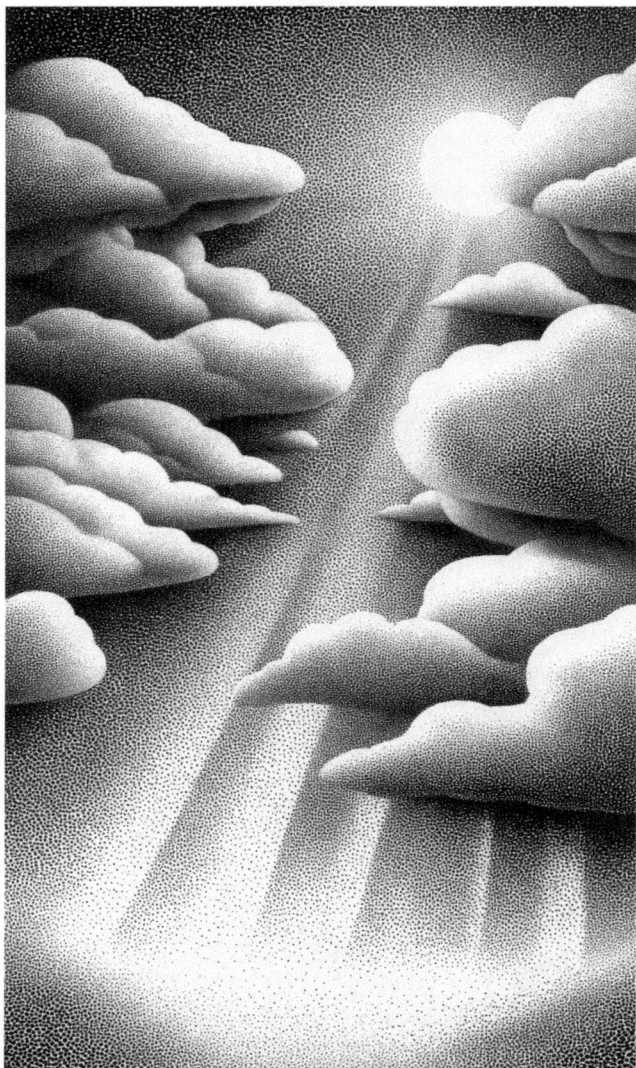

You are not the passing clouds of thought,
but the vastness they drift through.

CHAPTER 8

THE SELF IS PURE AWARENESS

Everything you've ever experienced has appeared in the same space. Not a physical space, but the inner openness where thoughts, feelings, and sensations come and go.

That space — clear, silent, untouched — is you.

The Witness Stands Alone

You've seen the body change. You've watched the mind change. Yet something hasn't moved an inch.

That still point isn't a thing or a location; it's the light of awareness by which all things are known.

You can't find it because it's what's doing the finding.

You can't see it because it's what makes seeing possible.

When Vedanta says, "You are awareness," it isn't

offering a belief. It's making a factual statement about your experience.

Awareness is the only constant you can never step outside of.

The Three States

You pass through three states every day — waking, dream, and deep sleep.

The waking world feels solid, the dream feels real until you wake, and in deep sleep everything disappears. Yet you say, "I slept well." That means something witnessed the absence of experience itself.

Awareness doesn't come and go with states. It illumines each in turn, like sunlight falling on different landscapes through the day.

When Vedanta says awareness is unbroken, it means it's the same "I" present through all three.

The Nature of Awareness

Awareness is not an object. It can't be measured or described. But we can understand its characteristics through negation:

Unchanging: All change appears in it, but it doesn't change.

Limitless: It has no boundary or location.

Self-revealing: It doesn't need another light to know itself.

Ever-present: It's never absent — not in sleep, not in death, not even in ignorance.

Everything else borrows existence from it. Awareness borrows from nothing.

Not a State of Mind

People sometimes think awareness is a meditative state, a special silence or bliss they can reach. But that's just another experience — something that begins and ends.

Awareness isn't an experience. It's that by which all experiences are known.

When the mind is calm, awareness is reflected clearly, like the moon reflected in still water. When the mind is busy, the reflection shakes but the moon hasn't changed.

Recognizing this frees you from chasing temporary peace. Peace was never lost; it was simply obscured by identification.

The Identity of the Individual and the Total

Vedanta makes a final, astonishing claim: the individual consciousness (atman) and total consciousness (Brahman) are not two. Like space inside a pot and space outside, they appear separate only by boundary.

Break the pot, and you realize there was never any division.

You were never a wave lost at sea. You were always the ocean itself.

Freedom Is Knowing What You Are

When this knowledge settles, life continues as before, but the center is gone. There's no longer a separate self managing the show, only the natural flow of the whole.

Action still happens, speech still happens, thoughts still happen, but they happen in awareness, not to someone.

This is freedom: not the end of life, but the end of misunderstanding.

You don't merge with awareness, you recognize you were never apart.

Freedom isn't something you achieve.
It's what remains when ignorance ends.

CHAPTER 9

FREEDOM IN KNOWLEDGE

When most people hear the word "enlightenment," they imagine a life-changing event — an explosion of bliss, an otherworldly vision, or a lightning bolt of divine grace. Vedanta says it's much simpler: freedom is knowledge.

Not knowledge about something, but the clear recognition of what you've always been. Experience comes and goes; knowledge stays.

If realization depended on a certain experience, it would vanish when the experience ended. But awareness — the knower of all experience — never disappears. Knowing that is liberation.

The End of the Seeker

The spiritual search begins with a simple belief: "I'm incomplete, and if I work hard enough, meditate long enough, or suffer nobly enough, I'll become complete."

The search ends when you see that completeness was never missing.

Freedom doesn't arrive; it's uncovered. The seeker doesn't become free. The seeker dissolves in the understanding that there was never anyone bound.

You can't reach yourself; you can only stop mistaking yourself for what you're not.

Freedom While Living

Vedanta calls this understanding *jivanmukti* — freedom while living. It doesn't mean floating above the world in a halo of detachment. It means knowing, even in the midst of chaos, that nothing real can be threatened.

The body still acts, the mind still reacts, the world still moves, but you know they are appearances within you, not definitions of you.

Suffering may visit, but it no longer stays. You can watch it come and go the way you'd watch a passing storm — present, yet never touching the sky itself.

The Quiet End of Seeking

After realization, life doesn't turn into perpetual bliss; it turns into peace. Not the peace of absence, but the peace of understanding.

There's no need to improve yourself or repair the world to feel whole.

Action still happens, but it's no longer driven by hunger or fear. You act because action is natural, not because you need the result to complete you.

This is what Vedanta means when it says karma ends in knowledge. You still continue to carry out actions — because you must — but that action no longer defines who you are.

The Disappearance of the Question

When ignorance is gone, even the question "Who am I?" fades. Not because it was answered with words, but because the one who was asking is gone.

The river merges with the ocean and stops calling itself a river. The wave realizes it was water all along.

That's why the sages smile quietly when asked about enlightenment. They aren't holding a secret, they're simply living in the obvious.

Freedom Is Your Nature

What Vedanta reveals is not a transformation but a recognition: you were never bound, never broken, never apart.

Freedom isn't found in the world; it's the ground of everything that appears in it. It's not a feeling or a state. It's your very being.

And once that's known, the game of becoming ends.

You can finally rest as what you've always been: pure, silent, self-luminous awareness.

PART 4

LIVING THE KNOWLEDGE

Knowing the truth isn't the end of the journey,
it's when the real understanding begins.

CHAPTER 10

FROM CONCEPT TO CLARITY

You can understand that you are awareness and still feel like a person. That's normal. The mind has spent a lifetime identifying with body, story, and struggle. It doesn't drop the habit just because you had an insight.

The truth may be instantaneous, but assimilation takes time. Knowledge must filter through every layer of thought and emotion until even your reflexes align with it.

Vedanta calls this stage *nididhyasana* — not meditation in the usual sense, but a gentle reconditioning of the mind until it lives from what it knows.

The Echo of the Old Program

Even after seeing clearly, old patterns echo. A thought arises — *I'm not good enough* — and for a moment, the old program runs again.

You may find yourself defending, judging, chasing,

avoiding. It's like waking from a dream but still half believing it. The dream's logic lingers.

This is why Vedanta never says "realization" happens once and for all. It's a process of dissolving residual ignorance, not adding new enlightenment. You aren't trying to gain the Self; you're learning to stop forgetting it.

The Obstacles: Vasanas and Emotion

What resists knowledge isn't the intellect, it's *vasanas*: deep-seated tendencies shaped by years of habit and experience. They're like grooves in the record of the mind. Even after the tune changes, the needle keeps slipping back into familiar tracks.

Emotions, too, can pull you out of clarity. Anger, grief, fear — they all narrow the field of awareness until you seem small again.

The key is not suppression, but understanding. Each wave of emotion rises and falls in you. The mistake is thinking it defines you. Let feelings pass through, but don't build a house in them.

Reconditioning Through Understanding

Assimilation isn't about discipline or austerity. It's about remembrance. Each time the mind forgets, you remind it: *This too appears in me.* Over time, the reminder becomes natural, effortless, almost automatic.

This is what Vedanta means when it speaks of "stabilizing knowledge." It's not a second realization; it's the deep rest that comes when the mind stops arguing with truth.

Practice Without a Practitioner

You can't "do" assimilation any more than you can "do" awareness. But the mind can cooperate. It can expose itself to truth again and again, through study, contemplation, and the company of those who live it.

You don't need to chase experiences or fight thoughts.

Just see each arising for what it is: another wave on the surface of the same ocean. In that seeing, everything slowly aligns.

The Mind Settles into Silence

Eventually, knowledge and mind become one.

The teachings that once felt like ideas turn into recognition.

You stop rehearsing them; you are them.

This is what peace looks like in Vedanta — not the absence of motion, but the absence of confusion. The mind still thinks, feels, acts — but it no longer imagines itself as the doer.

In that silence, life continues. But the one who suffered through it is gone.

Freedom doesn't change what you do,
it changes what you know yourself to be while doing it.

CHAPTER 11

THE WISE LIFE

Realization doesn't erase the world.

Bills still arrive. Bodies still age. Traffic still crawls.

But something fundamental shifts: you no longer expect life to deliver completion.

When you stop demanding that the world make you whole, you're free to engage it without fear or need.

The body acts, the mind reacts, but the Self — the awareness in which both appear — remains untouched. That simple shift transforms ordinary living into the wise life.

Spontaneous Dharma

From knowledge comes order.

When you know you aren't separate from the total, kindness and restraint stop being moral obligations. They become natural responses.

You don't help others to be good; you help because there are no others in the way you once imagined.

Compassion becomes sanity. Integrity becomes ease.

This is *dharma* in its highest form — not a set of rules, but harmony with what is.

No More Doership

The wise person still acts but doesn't carry the burden of authorship. Events unfold according to causes and conditions, and the body-mind simply participates in the flow.

When praise or blame comes, they land where they belong — in the field of appearances, not on you. You still move, decide, and respond —but with the lightness of knowing none of it defines you.

Emotions Without Ownership

Even the enlightened mind feels emotions. The difference is that wisdom ends possession.

Anger can arise, but it doesn't become my anger. Sadness can visit, but it isn't my tragedy.

You experience everything, yet remain untouched.

It's like watching weather move across a vast sky — never denying the storm, never mistaking yourself for it.

Enjoyment Without Attachment

The wise person enjoys life fully — music, conversation, nature, love— but without clinging. Pleasure is no longer chased; it's received and released.

This is the subtle joy Vedanta calls *ananda*: not excitement, but satisfaction. It's the happiness that doesn't depend on circumstances, because it flows from knowing you were never incomplete to begin with.

Freedom in Plain Sight

To the outside world, the wise life looks ordinary. There's no halo, no robe, no constant state of bliss. There's just a quiet ease in the midst of it all.

That's the real miracle: nothing changes except the illusion that anything needed to.

Freedom isn't on a mountaintop or in a monastery.

It's right here, walking the same streets, speaking the same words, only without the old confusion of who's living it.

The Gift of Clarity

The final expression of wisdom is gratitude.

Not the sentimental kind, but a deep recognition that everything — every pleasure, pain, loss, and longing— was part of the unveiling.

Life never needed fixing. It only needed understanding.

And in that understanding, you see that awareness was never separate from what it witnessed. The mirror was always clean. You just stopped noticing your own reflection long enough to see through it.

THE FIRST AND FINAL QUESTION

At the start of this book, we asked the question that has haunted humanity for millennia: *Who am I?*

By now, you've seen that it was never a question about identity, but about reality itself.

The search began with confusion — a self imagined as body, mind, story. It ends in the simple recognition that what you truly are was never touched by any of it. The world changed, thoughts changed, emotions came and went, but you — awareness — remained unchanged.

That realization doesn't erase the person you appear to be. It simply places the person in context: a fleeting reflection in a still lake.

The Quiet End of Becoming

Every journey of seeking is fueled by the belief that something is missing. When that belief dissolves, the search itself dissolves. Not because you've "found" something, but because there's nothing left to look for.

The wave doesn't reach the ocean; it recognizes it was never apart. Freedom isn't a destination — it's the collapse of distance.

When you know who you are, "becoming" ends in being.

Grace and Understanding

Vedanta calls the opportunity to hear these teachings shravana, and the moment they land — when they truly strike the heart — *anugraha*, grace. Grace isn't something given; it's the natural result of readiness meeting truth.

If this book found you, it's because you were already leaning toward what's real. Vedanta doesn't convert; it clarifies. And clarity, once seen, can't be unseen.

Living from Wholeness

Life continues. The body wakes, works, eats, sleeps. The world keeps turning. But inside, something is still.

The same awareness that watched childhood now watches adulthood, the same awareness that saw ignorance now witnesses understanding.

This continuity is you. It was never born, and it doesn't end.

To live from that knowing is the highest form of worship — not to something outside you, but to the truth of what you are.

The Question That Remains

And so the first question becomes the final one.

Not "Who am I?" asked in confusion — but "Who am I?" asked in wonder.

Not as a problem to solve, but as a living recognition that keeps deepening each moment.

Because what you are is not an idea, but the very awareness in which all ideas appear.

It can't be found because it was never lost. It can only be remembered — again and again — until even remembering falls silent.

A NOTE FROM
THE AUTHOR

You've reached the end of this book, but not the end
of the teaching.

Vedanta doesn't end in a single insight or a single text.
It unfolds as a way of seeing, again and again, until it
becomes the natural way you meet life.

If this book helped you glimpse that stillness behind
all movement, then it's done its work. Vedanta isn't
something to believe; it's something to understand —
and understanding begins with listening.

The next time you catch yourself reacting, rushing,
or resisting, pause and remember: Everything you
experience, you experience in awareness.

If you keep turning back to that, the teachings will
take root on their own. The mind will calm, the heart
will soften, and the world will seem less like a maze
and more like a mirror.

This is only Book One. Future volumes will explore

what this understanding means for how we live, act, and relate — how freedom expresses itself in the everyday.

But for now, rest.

Not as an instruction, but as a recognition. The search can finally end in what was here all along.

COMMON QUESTIONS AND MISUNDERSTANDINGS

Q: Is Vedanta a religion?

No. Vedanta isn't based on belief or worship. It's a means of knowledge — a method for removing ignorance about who you really are.

You can be of any faith (or none) and still benefit from it. Vedanta doesn't replace your worldview; it clarifies the ground beneath it.

––––––

Q: Does Vedanta require meditation?

Meditation can help prepare the mind, but it isn't the method itself. Vedanta is primarily an inquiry — a process of listening, reflecting, and assimilating the truth that your nature is already whole. You don't meditate to become awareness; you understand that you already are it.

––––––

Q: If I'm already free, why don't I feel free?

Because freedom is veiled by ignorance. You've mistaken the changing body, mind, and world for yourself. Once that misunderstanding is removed, freedom isn't gained — it's revealed.

———

Q: What about enlightenment experiences?

Experiences come and go. What you are is constant.

The peace of Vedanta isn't an experience to chase; it's the recognition that even your experiences happen in you, awareness. The highest experience still fades — knowledge doesn't.

———

Q: Does Vedanta reject the world?

Not at all. It simply points out that the world is dependently real — it exists, but it's not independent of consciousness. When you know yourself as awareness, you can fully engage the world without being trapped by it.

———

Q: Is there still a "person" after realization?

Yes, but only as a functional appearance — a name and form through which consciousness expresses itself. The body and mind continue to act according to their nature, but the sense of doership and limitation falls away. The "person" remains as a useful costume, not a prison.

———

Q: Do I need a teacher?

A qualified teacher helps you see what you can't see alone — the blind spot of self-identification. Books can open the door, but the mirror of a living teacher can show you exactly where misunderstanding hides.

That said, sincerity and consistent reflection can take you far.

———

Q: What happens after liberation?

Nothing happens — that's the point. Liberation isn't an event or an experience. It's the quiet understanding that you were never bound in the first place.

No lightning bolt, no permanent bliss, no new identity called "enlightened." The person doesn't vanish; it's simply seen for what it is — a passing appearance in awareness.

Life goes on exactly as before, but the feeling of me at the center of it dissolves. What's left is peace, clarity, and a natural lightness. The search ends, but living continues.

GLOSSARY OF TERMS

Adhyaropa–Apavada — The method of "superimposition and negation"; temporarily assuming what isn't true to reveal what is.

Atman — The true Self; the pure awareness that underlies all experience. Not the body, not the mind, but that which knows them.

Ananda — Bliss or fullness; not emotional pleasure, but the quiet satisfaction of completeness.

Avidya — Ignorance; the root cause of identification with the body and mind.

Brahman — The limitless reality, pure consciousness itself. Everything that exists appears within it.

Dharma — The natural order; living in harmony with truth, ethics, and one's role.

Guru — A teacher who transmits self-knowledge, not beliefs. The word literally means "the one who removes darkness."

Jiva — The individual soul or apparent person; awareness identified with body-mind.

Jivanmukti — Liberation while living; freedom from bondage to mind and circumstances.

Karma — Action and its results. In Vedanta, karma doesn't bind unless taken personally.

Maya — The power of illusion; the cosmic principle that makes the One appear as many.

Moksha — Liberation or freedom from ignorance; the goal of Vedanta.

Nididhyasana — Deep reflection or contemplation; the process by which knowledge becomes fully assimilated.

Satya — The real; that which is unchanging and independent, i.e., awareness.

Shravana — Listening; the first stage of Vedantic study, hearing the truth from a reliable source.

Vasana — A mental tendency or habit born of past experience; what keeps the mind restless and patterned.

Viveka — Discrimination; the ability to distinguish the real (unchanging) from the unreal (changing).

Vyavahara — The transactional or empirical world; everyday reality, valid for practical purposes but not ultimately real.

Daniel McKenzie's work explores the meeting point of ancient wisdom and modern life.

Through his long study of traditional Advaita Vedanta, he aims to communicate its timeless insights in plain, accessible language — not as philosophy, but as practical knowledge for self-understanding.

His notable works include *Samsara: An Exploration of the Hidden Forces that Shape and Bind Us*, where he examines the multifaceted concept of samsara, and *The Wisdom Teachings of the Bhagavad Gita*, a commentary that seeks to unlock the *Gita's* teachings in accessible terms.

His ongoing project, **The Broken Tusk**, is an online collection of essays, stories, and a growing Vedanta glossary written for contemporary seekers.

To learn more, visit **www.thebrokentusk.com**

The "Vedanta in Plain English" Series

Book 1 - Who Am I, Really?
An Ancient Guide to Self-Knowledge

Forthcoming
Book 2 - Why the World Feels So Real
Understanding Perception Through Vedanta

Forthcoming
Book 3 - The Order of Things
A Vedantic Look at Karma and Causation

Forthcoming
Book 4 - Living Wisely
How to Find Equanimity in a Changing World

Forthcoming
Book 5 - Freedom Without Escape
The End of Seeking and the Discovery of Peace